TO P9-DXJ-611

tiNA

Best Wishes

Artone —

Tina
God Bless you
Elsie

Elsie

ANTONIA G. ROJAS

authorHOUSE®

AuthorHouse™
1663 Liberty Drive
Bloomington, IN 47403
www.authorhouse.com
Phone: 1-800-839-8640

Published by AuthorHouse 5/16/2012

ISBN: 978-1-4685-8019-8 (sc)
ISBN: 978-1-4685-8018-1 (e)

THIS BOOK IS DEDICATED TO MY FRIEND CONNIE.

FOREVER IN OUR HEARTS.

Seven Teenagers in the House

$\mathcal{EO}$ - This thought came to me quite often in 1967. I couldn't believe that I was the mom of 7 teenagers. There were some blessings in disguise; the boys socks were about the same size, this made sorting easier. They could help each other with homework, and there were enough chores for everyone.

Now the girls had to have a mirror handy to apply mascara, and that blue eye shadow. (I see some of you remember by the smiles on your face.) My girls were in style with their nylons and of course the girdles were a necessary part of their everyday wardrobe. Not to mention the hair curlers dripping with dippy do.

AR - Elsie, what would women today do if they had to wear girdles to be a fashion statement? For crying out loud!! (kind of a fun expression, for crying out loud.)

EO - I don't think women would wear girdles. It was very uncomfortable. A person could not breathe. This would turn us into *Desperate Housewives.*

AR-How long did you have seven teenagers in the house?

EO-The seven teenager stage didn't last extremely long. About three months because my Virgie turned 20. I look back to those years filled with so many precious moments, a lifetime of love in action.

AR - Can we start at the beginning of the Olivas Family?

EO - I will have much to say about those teenage years, probably at least two more chapters.

AR - Anytime you want to talk about 1967, we can do that.

Tom Serves Our Country

EO- Tave and his brother Ernie served in the U.S. Army. Ernie and Tave had not seen each other during their deployment. Letter writing was not a reliable method of communication.

One day, Tave was told, that he had company waiting. What a surprise when the two brothers saw each other. It had to be wonderful when the two brothers embraced.

My mother-in-law said she prayed every day for their safe return, and was so proud when they both returned with an honorable discharge

AR- The Olivas family must wave their flags high on Veterans Day. Such pride in a father named Tom.

EO- I am thankful my kids knew about their dad's service to his country. And we have had many of our family members serve in the military. No words are necessary to express our gratitude. A mother's prayers once again answered.

Man Named Tom

EO- Nineteen forty-seven was when my eyes first saw Tom Olivas. I lived in Greeley on 2nd Avenue with my sister Edda and her husband Antonio. Our community was a small farming community that labored in the fields to earn a living.

There were potatoes, sugar beets, and onion fields in abundance. The laborers worked long hours, with no protection from the sun.

The pay was about .35 cents per basket of produce. Onions were picked and put into 50 pound bags. Sugar beets were large and heavy to lift. The potatoes were stored in cellars.

AR-Once, in Greeley, I saw a pickle dock, where a huge truck unloaded pickles into this huge barrel, and they cured the pickles in a brine. I have also lived near a sugar beet factory, where you could smell the beets cooking. The smell was very rich, and strong.

One time the syrup from the sugar beets spilled outside onto the streets. Our town made national news, but I mostly remember cars getting stuck in the syrup. What a sight-for a change there was a traffic jam, not because of ice on the streets.

Today we still have migrant farm workers. Their average earnings are $7500 per year. Labor laws have helped improve housing and working conditions. There is still a need for labor laws to protect young children from being in the fields and health insurance for the workers.

A generation still dreaming of a better life for their kids. Someday, I would like to follow a crop of tomatoes, from seed to market. The time, the cost, the labor involved for one tomato- a valuable experiment.

This process of planting a crop, weeding it, and harvesting is an investment of time, effort and money. There are no guarantees that seed is going to germinate.

A seed is planted and we wait in anticipation to watch the tiny sprout bursting with promise. (fresh salsa) Corn on the cob, lathered in butter, or cucumbers sliced and a squeeze of lemon juice added with salt, what goodness.

A Seed is Planted

A seed is so very small,
Will it grow to be tall,
Will I take the time to watch it grow?
What seeds will I sow?

What hope have I in this little seed,
Knowing it's me, someday it will feed.
With plenty of water and hot sunshine,
To burst forward with flavor in its due time.

EO- We always had food to eat, and we would store potatoes, chili, and beans. So add some tortillas and our meals were complete. Sometimes we had lamb, or beef to cook.

AR-Elsie, Today these same items are on our menu. Except now we can buy tortillas. The price of lamb is about $10 per pound.

I remember walking into your house and there was always something cooking. The smell of homemade tortillas greeted us at the door. It was a stack about ten inches high. That is before the kids helped themselves to a fresh tortilla.

(I hope everyone can experience eating a warm tortilla hot off the press, and if you have, give the woman cooking them a hug.)

Sometimes they were lathered with butter or peanut butter. Sunday dinners were pot roast with plenty of mash potatoes. (probably at least a 5 pound bag) I can't remember the last time I saw someone peeling potatoes. Can you? For that matter how about hanging laundry out to dry?

Remembrance

I take Elsie's hand in mine,
I ask her how many tortillas did you make
How many cakes did you bake?

How many jeans did you wash,
She looks at me and says-Oh my gosh.
How many tender words did you speak,
From a heart so humble and meek.

A R- I remember you always had company show up at a moments notice. You always made us feel welcomed and immediately made coffee. The families were not small, our family had seven, and add your family of nine.

You cooked a meal for sixteen people with lots of love and ease. I would like to imagine that you today, could have your own cooking show.

We could have a huge pot of coffee and it would be called, The Essence of Elsie - what do you think? Or perhaps *Eloisa's Cocina?*

EO- I don't know about that. I do enjoy watching my TV shows - The Young and the Restless, and the Spanish channel has a show called-Casos de Familia.

It is based on true events of everyday life. Today, there are many cooking shows.

AR-I just had another thought, the cooking show could also be seen on the Spanish channels, because you are bilingual.

Your viewers would include so many family and friends, as they sat down to watch *ELOISIA'S COCINA.*

I have a recipe that is so vivid in my mind. Can you imagine Elsie, the state of Wyoming having a Spanish cooking show???

EO-That would be something else huh. What is the recipe that you speak of?

AR-I remember visiting your family and you had a special dessert. It was a cake, but Elsie, you added your touch.

A fresh pot of coffee would be perking, as you cut each person a piece. You would cut a piece of cake and poke holes in it.

Then milk from a can would be poured into the holes. As a child, this was such a very rare occurrence. You savored every bite, with your coffee in hand.

Today, there is a cake called - pastel de tres leches. It has three different kinds of cream. It sells for about three dollars a slice. You knew it was something special then; Elsie's Pastel con Leche. Do you still enjoy this special treat?

EO-Every now and then- I enjoy a warm piece of cake. Carnation milk was what I poured into my piece of cake.

My idea was to keep it moist. I continue to use the carnation milk to make my gravy. I always had all the ingredients handy, and the kids loved cake. I also fed my babies carnation milk. Growing up, we did not have a refrigerator, so canned milk was a necessity. Today the price of a can of milk is over a dollar. Sure has gotten expensive.

AR- Today, someone will ask for a recipe and they will say, that it is a family recipe and it is a secret.

EO-No secret recipe, it was just plain chocolate cake.

AR-Did anyone notice your special pastel con leche?

EO-Just you!!!

AR-Elsie, can't you see it in your mind:

Eloisa's Cocina

Today - Pastel con Leche
Fresh pot of coffee
Free sample to be included
No secret recipe…

EO- For this cooking show of *ELOISA'S COCINA* could we get some new pans, mine are quite used from cooking for seven children. Pans now a days come in such bright colors. However, I need to practice first because each oven heats different. I would not want to burn the cake on national TV.

AR-*ELOISA'S COCINA* will be stocked with the best of cooking utensils. What makes *ELOISA'S COCINA* is you. Thank you for allowing me to imagine a place for you…. *ELOISA'S COCINA.*

EO-I was imagining my kitchen also, perhaps I could have a phone close by, just in case family called.

AR-Upon a visit to see Elsie, my sister Jenny came along with her comal and masa harina. (comal is a griddle) All of a sudden *ELOISA'S COCINA* was open for business.

We could hear the humming of the pressure cooker in the background.

The last time I heard a pressure cooker was about 30 years ago. Sometimes a person will say, that their life is like a pressure cooker.

Today we have slow cookers. Interesting that we went from pressure cookers to slow cookers! When was the last time you heard a pressure cooker?

Interview: We have a special guest in *ELOISA'S COCINA* today. Our special guest is Jenny Gonzales from Colorado, formerly from Medicine Bow, Wyoming. (She wanted to say she was Rachael Ray!)

Miss Jenny, how long have you been making gorditas?

JG-I would like to say all of my life, because my kids love them, my grandkids request gorditas stuffed with eggs for breakfast. The Masa Harina can be purchased in any grocery store.

EO-Well we can buy it in Laramie, but not in Rock River. I know that for sure.

During this wonderful visit, Elsie prepared green-chili, and a fresh pot of beans. There was at least a dozen of gorditas which I stuffed and put on the table.

Elsie looked at them and said - Neto- I haven't had gorditas for at least forty years. *ELOISA'S COCINA* experienced a new recipe: gorditas. If you haven't tasted a gordita, you have missed a treat. Gordita means someone who is plump!

Elsie and Emma put honey and butter on their gorditas. I wonder how they taste with cinnamon?

Elsie commented that if her relatives called, she was going to make sure they knew what was cooking. Five minutes later, the phone rang, and gorditas were the hot topic.

Elsie's favorite meal is spare ribs, and freshly cooked beans. Victor likes noodles, pasta, macaroni and cheese.

I asked Elsie why pasta. She said that she told her kids she was Italian because her last name was Vergel. (Vigil in Spanish) We all know how kids remind us of our words in a convenient time.

Well, Elise had not voted for three years. She received a notice in the mail, informing her that she was being deported because she had not voted.

Well, David turned to Elsie and told her, "Well mom, now we can go to Italy."

EO-I was just kidding, but David believed we were Italian!

FYI - Hospitality- Elsie has the gift of hospitality. She shares her home, and gives you a place to be yourself and belong.

She does not focus on what a person wears, make-up, or jewelry. Her main purpose is to share her time and her heart.

AR-What would you like your kids to know about you?

EO-I think they know everything there is to know about me. I just want them to know that I love them very much.

Which reminds me of the hobos that got off the trains and walked over to our house. I wondered if they knew they were loved. They were dirty, tired, hungry, and scary.

Baked bread was a temptation for a hobo that came to our home. Perhaps the smell of the bread drew him inside.

He came in the front door, and I quickly gathered my kids and ran out the back door.

Another time, a hobo made his presence known, but this time my Victor was prepared. He grabbed the twenty two, but he did not have a steady hand. He had the gun pointed at Virgie. That was scarier than the hobo being in our home!

Another time, a very special request was granted by Tave. I had seen a hobo inside an old building. Well Tave went to check on him. I prayed for Tave and the Hobo.

He came back with a strange request. The man wanted a can of sardines and an onion. Go figure huh. What would be our request if we hadn't eaten in three days?

AR-We did see plenty of hobos especially during the summer months. I was very frightened because they just walked right into our home. Perhaps they were homeless people that traveled by train. I also wondered about their lives.

Did their families worry about them? Where did they spend Christmas? I would like to interview a hobo and tell his stories someday.

I did some research and discovered that during the depression, men traveled by train to look for employment. To some men it was a choice, and they didn't have to worry about paying bills, or the price of gas or groceries. They called it riding the rails.

Flashback Candy Bars

Bazooka bubble gum-with comics inside.

Fruit strip gum- stripes on the piece of gum

Kool-Aid - 1975 -our mouths, teeth, and tongues turned
so many colors

Pringles potato chips-a potato was pressed and formed
a chip

Big hunk candy bar-white nugget -turned our mouth
white, and almost pulled our teeth out.

Black licorice-this turned our teeth black

Penny candy-today they cost a dime

Special drink- A & W root beer floats, better than all
the sodas on the market today.

Elise's favorite candy is: Payday, and Mr. Goodbar, and
peanuts.

Elsie's Journey

EO- I grew up surround by some first class cooks. My sister Edda was the one who raised me, because my mom died when I was nine. My family lived in New Mexico, close to Mora.

AR- A life changing event at the age of 9. What happened to your mom, and what was her name?

EO- My mom's name is Virginia. My Virgie is named after her. My father's name is Ezikel. My mom named me Maria Eloisa. My siblings are: Edda, Pablo, and Emelia, Josefita, Felones, Ezikeil, Purfie and Ignacita.

EO-I remember my mom being sick in bed. I would go to her room and build a fire so she would be warm. I wanted to comfort her, but at the age of 9, was not too sure what would make her feel better. I was told she had cancer, but no one told me she would die from this disease- perhaps they were protecting me.

I don't know what a child of 9 can do if she knows her mom is dying. Sometimes we lit a candle, we cried, we prayed and we held each other tight.

Butterflies in October

EO - My whole family grieved for my mom, I remember the day she died. I walked in and the adults were standing around her. Her face was covered with a towel, and I wanted to remove it so I could see if she was breathing. A solution that made sense to a child of 9.

She was sick for about a year. She had a wound and this caused her excruciating pain, and she would cry.

My mom passed away in the early morning. I don't know if I heard this, or glanced at the clock. Just amazing what a young heart remembers.

It was towards the end of October when we buried her. I don't remember being present at the funeral but I heard an amazing story. Several persons spoke about what had happened. They said that beautiful butterflies circled her coffin, not just one mind you. There were several butterflies.

Here it was the end of October, and very cold. As a child I would image the butterflies carrying my mom to heaven. This thought helped me because I knew she wasn't alone.

AR-My mom died when I was 6, I remember being at her funeral but did not know the significance of the death of a mother. How can a child put words to what they are feeling? Children grieve in brief moments, and then they are off playing. The next day, the reality makes its presence known.

Anger, and questioning God becomes a way of life. No answers appear in the horizon. I think we learn to live with the absence of our loved one, but from that day forward our days are never the same.

Each of us process grief in a different way, in our own time. It is a sacred passage. Losing my mom at the age of six, allows me to embrace Elsie and say, I know how it feels. Sometimes a song, a photo, music can send us back to our aching heart.

Nothing stops the sun from arriving each new day. We are grateful to be awaken by birds singing, or snow gently falling. Once again we realize we are not in control.

Today

I haven't seen my mom today, So many people speaking
    softly, I can't hear what they say.
When will she return I ask, No one answers, the silent
    lasts.
I want to hear her voice tomorrow,
Because around me is so much sorrow.
My Grama holds her hankie tight, I hear her crying
    through the night. I haven't seen my mom today,
And now it's me that needs to pray.
Please let her hold me for one more day.

Dr. Wolfelt said: Anyone who is old enough to love, is old enough to grieve.

EO-Because of my mom's illness, I went to stay with my Grama and her sister Juanita.

My aunt Juanita had her bedtime routine, like brushing our teeth. In the evening, she would warm water and get a wash cloth. She would wash her hands and face. Soon it was my turn, and very gently she would do the same.

But the routine was not over, she would open a small

round container that had a rose on the lid, and she would put salve on my hands and face. The salve soothed my skin, and the fragrance was not overpowering. I remember watching her eyes as she smiled at me. Well, I mean I was a small child, but I sure do remember feeling like I had been rolled up in a very warm blanket !!!!

I remember doing something that seems funny now. It helped the night not seem so scary. My Grama's house had walls and ceilings that were made out of dirt. At night I could see the dirt fall on my sheets. I held my hands out, as if to receive a gift from heaven. A gentle sprinkle fell softly like it was snowing dirt. I felt like this was my secret to keep, because perhaps others would tell me that it was just only dirt.

The evenings were welcomed with prayer from her bible. At times the kids in the neighborhood would say that she was a witch who prayed from a black book. Well her bible was black, and because the kids didn't know- they made something up. I wish they could have heard my Grama's prayers about Christ love for each of us.

My sibling and I also stayed with my sister Felones. We sat in these long benches, like the Waltons, all thirteen of us. Our meals were simple and we always had enough to feed each person.

I remember passing around jelly to put on freshly baked bread. The talk around the table was different every night. Sometimes the boys talked about the sling shots they had designed, and we heard about the produce in the garden.

Evening prayer was never skipped. We prayed at Gramas house and at my mother's house, so it was a part of our evening routine.

I remember something unusual about Avelino, Felones husband. After our evening meal, we would eat pinion. Since Avelino wore false teeth, we handed our peeled pinion over to him. There were thirteen of us peeling so we peeled faster than what he could eat! The things we remember- huh.

I was surrounded by women who demonstrated their faith by the way they lived their life. Raising a family on limited resources encouraged each person to be creative, and to contribute something. There is always something to give back.

It was easy for me to pray, and to feel God's love. My trust in God felt very normal, and I believed that my family belonged to Christ family. If we couldn't go to church, we would pray at home. The church was the building, and we brought life to the church.

As youngster all my children went to church, I didn't question my faith for one moment. I was very young, and missed my mom desperately, so my faith gave me hope. I continued to grow and seek my Christ every day. He has walked by my side through the pain, disappointments, and heartaches.

AR- Nobody promised us a boat on the ocean, without any waves. Life is about change, and acceptance. When my children were young they wanted to know why this or why that. Well, I didn't have the answer then and today, my reply is the same- I don't know.

EO-We have to be at peace with some questions that can't be answered. I know that there are times that I can't sleep, and I refuse to take sleeping pills. I tell everyone that my sleeping pill is strong, long lasting, and I never have to buy a prescription. It is my prayers.

Being a mom brought new worries; mine were worries about Tave and seven children. I remember we received a notice about our taxes that needed to be paid. I worried about the dumb bill, and wondered where we would get the money.

Tave just said, we would sleep on it and see what we do the next day. How is it that some people snore like they don't have a care in the world?

I always felt I had to do something, so worrying was better than doing nothing. I don't remember how that dumb bill got paid, but it did!!!!

My prayers got answered in one way or another. I know my angels surround me daily, my part is to welcome them.

AR-Well Elsie, your faith is so strong, and comforting. I admire your strength through your journey. Heartache, and loss have been present. Do you think that faith is something that can be taught?

EO-My sisters prayed and talked about their faith, and I saw them extend their love to others. I watched them practice their faith, by the way they lived their life.

Our house was far from being perfect, but we could count on each other.

I also know that God makes his presence known to us through people, dreams, and circumstances.

Sacred Moments

EO- I lost my sons, Steven and George, but I have seen them in my dreams. George was stillborn, at the time of his birth. Steven and George were both in my dream. George had brown hair, and was a very husky man. My Steven loved the mountains, and in this vision they had their arms around each other, as they ran through the field.

As a mother, it filled my heart with joy, because I know we have eternal life. I also have dreams of Tave, where he very gently hugs me. This life gives us so many opportunities to believe.

AR-Our days are so turbulent, Elsie, that trusting God is like drinking water to quench our thirst- a necessity. I know you have a lifetime of faith in action.

EO-I remember so many, but this showed me how God knows our heart, and honors the smallest wishes.

Tave and I had gone to Loveland with his sister to pick cherries. It was an all-time favorite for the kids to enjoy this juicy fruit. We had to climb ladders to reach, so I was folding the ladder and my finger got caught. Tave helped me take the ring off, and it was all bent and smashed. Looked like someone had taken a hammer to it.

I sadly looked at my ring and thought that perhaps in the future, I could get another set.

Well, being a busy mom, time went by. I still envisioned my finger with a beautiful ring. (What woman doesn't think of jewelry?)

Anyway, my kids often spent their vacations with their cousins in Greeley. Going swimming was a summer time favorite. One day, David went swimming to the pool with his cousins.

At the pool, David felt something around his toe. You are probably guessing as to what he found. Yep it was an engagement ring. It had two crosses on the side. Well my brother-in-law Louie decided to turn it in so it could be returned to the owner.

They kept it for a while, and no one claimed it. Louie decided to give it to David since he had found it.

David was around 5 and did not have a need for an engagement ring, so he gave it to me -his mama. You know that ring fit me like it was mine all along. I still have it and it is beautiful.

Well, that is not the end of this story. Let me tell you how the other part of this set showed up. Working with the railroad, the families were required to move quite often. We were living in Harper, Wyoming and my kids went to school in Bosler, Wyoming. Students came from several towns to attend school.

My Victor was playing outside in the playground and saw something that caught his eye. Yep it was a beautiful gold band. Wow, to good to be true, huh. Well he was so excited, that he could hardly talk. His little boy smile was as bright as the ring!

I couldn't believe it myself, but it fit perfect. I put the band and then the engagement ring. I had my new wedding ring set.

I admired it, and felt like I had just gotten away with something, and not quite sure what!!!!

Well there you are, I had wished for a new wedding ring set, and just told myself….someday. Mind you, my patience was required.

Number one, the set fit me perfect. Number two, it had two crosses on the side, number three -they were free. Number four-I needed a new set. Number five-Who gives us the perfect gift? God puts everything within our reach.

AR- What a beautiful miracle. You could have been in all the fancy jewelry stores and never found a set designed especially for you.

I have to share a miracle story similar to yours, but doesn't involve diamonds.

My daughter Jeanette was in middle school when I asked her if she wanted to go to Hawaii to celebrate her graduation.

Hawaii wasn't on the radar for her as much as going to see the vampire state building, in New York. Well I told her it was the Empire state building, and Hawaii was beautiful during the summer.

We talked about it through the years, and the vampire state building was her choice.

You know how time catches up to us, and here we were in her senior year. She told me that she was entering a writing contest for a magazine.

She was so excited to tell me that the prize was $10,000. She asked for suggestions and I gave her a few, and off she went to write this article. Well, two months went by, and no communication was received.

She was having a very busy school year, and I thought it would keep her mind off the vampire state building!

Well, one day she called to tell me that our answering machine had a message that she had won. Five young women from across the United States had been selected. Jeanette was one of the young women invited to New York.

Flight, hotel and expenses were paid for two members of the family. Hawaii did not enter my mind!!!! We went and walked down time square, went to ground zero, and yes went to the Empire State building for free because she knew a friend from high school who worked there.

After we returned home, Jeanette saw our pictures at the Empire state building. She commented that her wish had come true, and she had a picture to remember to trust God.

For the last five years our discussion was about going to Hawaii, and she wanted to go see the vampire state building. God had answered her prayer plus added a $10,000 scholarship.

Every detail was taken care of. We even had a driver pick us up at the airport. I worried about having to drive in New York City!

EO-So you didn't have to drive in New York, I can image the traffic there. Well, let me tell you about my Steven's miracle.

My Steve was constantly throwing up, and could not hold any formula in his tummy. My fear was intense for my baby. We took him to Denver and we were referred to a heart specialist. The doctors told us they had found a tear close to his heart. I kneeled down to pray and asked for his restoration.

About a week later, we received a call from my brother that my father, Ezikel had passed away. Tave and I left to attend the funeral.

Before we left, I took a pair of my Steven's baby shoes; they were very small because he was about six months old. My thought was to take his shoes to El Santuario in New Mexico.

It is a small church about fifteen minutes from Santa Fe. About 200 years ago, a crucifix was unearthed at this location.

The church is made out of adobe, and is very old. No detailed architecture, or luscious gardens will be found.

There is a hole in the ground that looks like a well. The dirt in this hole is said to contain healing properties. Visitors are allowed to take holy dirt home.

Many travel to *El Santuario* in Chimayo, with a faithful heart. Many come to be restored, and to experience the humility of stepping on holy grounds.

El Santuario was referenced as sacred grounds where miracles were plentiful.

The church was small, the benches old, but the serenity that I felt lifted my sadness. Tave sat beside me as I prayed and wept. Before we left, I placed my Steven's shoes on the altar. I felt I had left my heart in this beautiful sacred building.

AR- I have been to *El Santurio* and the church is very simple, but beautiful. Silence is observed as each person brings their petitions to the altar. There are letters of testimonies, pictures, and lots of personal items. I noticed a special area with pictures of soldiers.

I wanted to go to *El Santurio* because I had read a beautiful story about a man who was blind and went to seek healing. He struggled with the simplicity of going to a church to pray for healing. Could it be this simple?

Well God restored his vision but in a profound way. He can see colors, and today is a famous painter. He is still blind, but he said that God healed him by giving him the gift of seeing colors. We never know how God will use our infirmities.

EO-I have heard so many stories, even as a child I wondered about a place called Chimayo. Why did God use such a humble setting so we can see his glory?

Well, Tave and I went back home to Wyoming. He had to go back to work, and I remember his check was short because of the time off. None the less, we had to focus on our family.

Steven had an appointment two weeks later with a heart specialist. I was very nervous, because the doctors had spoken about doing heart surgery.

There were about 7 doctors in the room. They were from California, New York, all over. Well, Tave and I waited as the doctors talked among themselves.

The group of doctors sat with us and told us they could not find anything wrong. The doctors looked at me and said, "You can spank him now."

The doctors had no explanation, and I didn't need one. I looked at Tave, and at my Steven and could see my baby's shoes at the altar. My son had been healed. I experienced God's grace in my son, Steven.

AR- Was Steve able to participate in sports?

EO- Oh yes, he was very active in school sports. We took Steven back to school, and he cried because he thought the school was the hospital. His brothers and sisters took special care of him, by carrying him piggy-back and giving him treats.

AR-Elsie, you really believed with all of you heart that your son would be healed?

EO- I did, with all of my heart and mind. I would like to tell you about another similar experience. I have some beautiful memories and as I speak, more and more come to mind.

AR- This is your story Elsie, so take it away. My aunt Francis uses this expression-take it away Lorenzo!!!

EO-Sounds like you have some special relatives too. Anyway, this one morning I went to get out of bed, and I could not walk. My hands were very tender. I told myself that it was laundry day, and much needed to be done.

We had a ringer washing machine and I had to put each piece of clothing through the ringer. I wanted to cry as I felt each piercing jab.

During supper Tave noticed that I was off balance. I showed him my hands and the swelling of my feet. Tave decided to seek medical attention. The doctors thought I had rheumatic fever. I called my family in Greeley and explained my condition.

My brother Tony, told me about an Indian friend who had learned to heal people from his Grama. Well, we drove to Greeley, with high expectations. I knew how I felt and needed some relief from the pain.

The coffee was ready for us and my sisters wanted to inspect my hands right away. Their concern was genuine, as they tried to diagnose my condition.

My brother told me they were going to build a fire in the wood stove and roast some cactus.

Tave and my siblings cut the cactus and were taking the thorns off one by one. I could see everyone so tense as they took this job very serious. I can clearly see Tave removing the stickers from the cactus and I love him even more.

My brother came inside with the roasted cactus and cut them open. Inside of each cactus was a gel; like the consistency of aloe vera gel. The cactus felt very warm as they placed them on my joints and on my feet and hands.

AR- Sounds like you looked like a lizard covered in green.

EO- I guess you can say that. This was the process for the next few days. Everyone held their breath as they helped me out of bed. The cheering that took place when I could walk again!!!

The love I felt from everyone, was also part of my healing. I was ready to go home and see my babies. My family cried as we said our goodbyes. I could tell that Tave wanted to return home and was so relieved to have a healthy wife.

Home Remedies

EO- Home remedies were a very strong method of healing our ailments. My sisters had their own home remedies and I also used them when my children were ill.

My sister Edda always kept apricot jam handy because she said it helped cut down a fever. I think a person has to believe in the remedies, otherwise why use them.

I know people will laugh, but I know they worked. I used bread and milk mixed together in a paste and rubbed on my niece Becky, who had stepped on a piece of glass. Well the next day her foot was fine. She told her mom that Aunt Elise fed her through the soles of her feet.

With seven children, what was a mother to do? Colds, coughs, and scrapes were plenty at our house. I would have been at the doctor's office at least once a week. I had watched my sister's tend to us by using family remedies. I guess you could call them hand me down remedies.

AR- I also have a list of hand me down remedies. My Grama would cut potatoes and soak them in vinegar. She insisted we lay down and she would put the potatoes around our forehead. The first time I saw this, the potatoes actually got dry. It was like the fever had cooked them. It made an impression on me because I was only eight.

EO-Traveling to town for an emergency didn't happen very often. So we had remedies to help us heal our hurts. But I have to stress the importance of our belief in wanting to be healed. Doctors have their place; they provide medical healings as well.

Role Models

AR- Who did you look up to growing up? Today we use the term role models.

EO-My sister Edda is the person who influenced me. I loved her so much, and her kindness was so very present. She would give me consejos along the way.

She told me not to scold kids in front of their friends or family. There would be another place and a time. My sister Edda had an effective way to discipline me. Whenever I got in trouble, (I can't imagine Elsie in trouble.) I had to explain to my friends why I couldn't play.

Of course everyone wanted to know why. Her response was, you must ask Elsie what she did to get in trouble. When a person actually admits what they did wrong to their friends…wow…Kinda makes you stop breathing!

AR-How did you know your sister Edda loved you?

EO- After the death of my mom, she asked my dad if I could live with her and husband Antonio. It could have been easy for her to go and raise her family, and leave me with my dad. But she thought about me. She said I belonged with her.

EO- My brother, Pablo said that Edda and I were *Las Cuatas,* which means twins. He said we were always together. She was about nine years older. She was my best friend, and an example of love.

My Grama, bless her soul, would give me an apple but my sisters did not get an apple. My sister Edda would cut slices so we could all enjoy our treat. How could I eat my apple in front of my sisters?

I was comfortable being a child around Edda. She bought paper dolls and allowed us leisure hours of play. One thing that is very special to me is that she wanted me to have curls in my hair. So much so, that she would perm it. It would take time and yes, it stunk up the whole house. But she wanted me to feel like a princess. I received so many compliments on my hair.

She got to know all of my children, and was so proud of the mom I had become.

Edda died at the age of 63, and when I think of her, it is the beautiful memories that linger in my heart. When it is all said and done this is what we leave.

Edda

I know that you were sent from above,
To comb my hair, to wipe my tears,
To be my mom through the years.

Because of you I learned to pray,
 and trust in the beginning of each new day.
Your love was tender, your words kind,
A mother's love in you I found.

You gave me a home where I belonged.
To be with family, to laugh, to sing, to cry,
And you helped me tell my mommy good-bye.

My words are not enough to say,
How much you blessed me each day.
I know that you were sent from above,
Forever grateful, for a heart so genuine.

What is Elsie's favorite color? - Red

Everyone in her family knows this fact. She also enjoys orange on a particular day during football season! We all know why, because of her Broncos.

Elsie's greatest fear-she was afraid to die and leave her children without their mommy. One of her sister's died all of sudden. The greatest time of fear was when Virgie turned eight. It was around the same age when she lost her mom.

Rumors of the end of the world caused Elsie some sleepless nights. She asked her daddy about this rumor and he told her to sit down and he would explain.

EO-My daddy said the world ended for a person when they died. The world started for a person when they were born. He said there would always be rumors about the end of the world, and he said the world ends and begins everyday for someone.

His explanation put my mind at ease, and yes there still are many rumors of the world ending. You can imagine how many times I have heard these rumors in my lifetime.

Friendship and Amistad

AR- Elsie, seems to me that Edda was your best friend. Friendships are so important in our lives. Especially when women get together and share their stories of their children, their pain, joys and of course we always talk about our weight! We always have so much to tell!

You left your family and moved to Wyoming as a married woman. Tell me about the friends you met in Wyoming.

EO-One person comes to mind right away. It is Ruth Mascarenas. She also lived in Wyoming and her husband Gaspar worked on the railroad with Tave.

I could smell her cooking from far away. She always had a beautiful garden and shared her produce with all the families.

I was the recipient of mansanilla tea. She would save me a huge bundle of this precious tea. Mansanilla tea is used to calm a person. I think of my friend and know how she brought calm into my life.

I know Ruth had my best interest at heart, because she listened intently. I valued our friendship because she made me laugh.

We saw each other at church on Sunday's and I admired her so much because she came an hour early to set-up and clean.

A priority for Ruth was attending adoration. This is a personal time of prayer and dedication.

Her children were in school with my children. Her children are Joan, Monica, Debbie and Eddie. We saw each other at basketball games and had a few minutes to visit.

AR-I remember Ruth, and her garden was boxed in with railroad ties. She wore a hat as she tended to her garden. Her eyes were as beautiful as the sunflowers that she grew. Her shelves were full of vegetables she had canned.

She invited me to see the Ed Sullivan show when the Beatles were on TV for the first time in the United States. Joan and I were glued to the TV and Ruth was in the kitchen preparing some snacks.

Her house was always so clean, but like a welcome clean, not squeaky clean. A person could sit on the couch and notice that the floors were always shiny.

EO-I remember one day that Lupe sent you to borrow clothespins from Ruth. The word you used was palitos and Ruth told you they were outside. She thought you were asking for wood kindling.

Some words have different meaning and you didn't know. We all learned a new word, especially since clothes can't be hung to dry with wood kindling.

Ruth taught me a lot about friendship. We nourished each other's faith. Life in the bitter cold was lonely at times. The bitter cold kept us inside, but when Ruth and I saw each other it was time to catch up. Living in Wyoming especially during winter would turn anyone into a-Desperate Housewife! It would be fun to have some of Hollywood desperate housewives move to Wyoming. I wonder what their hair do's would look like in our Wyoming wind!

AR-Walking with a friend in the dark, is better than walking in the dark alone-By Helen Keller

To Ruth

We were like two sister together, side by side our
    friendship grew.
I learned to trust God, and believe the truth, because of
    you, my Friend Ruth.
Through the years we calmed each other's fears, and
    treasured each other's tears.
We trusted each other with our deepest feelings, because
    of you, my life had meaning.
My wish for all, to find a treasure, in a friend whose love
    can't be measured.

Spanish Translations

EO - My family spoke Spanish, but after the death of my mom, I moved to Greeley with my sister. The transition was difficult because there was no time for me to learn English.

Every student's nightmare is to be called to the front of the class. Well it happened to me, only I didn't understand what the teacher was asking me to do. She told me to get a stool and come to the front and pull the map down.

My nephews always called each other stoolpigeon, which meant that someone was tattling. I understood the word pigeon, and started looking for a bird.

Well my friend Alice told the teacher that I didn't understand English. I was embarrassed because I was in the front of the class. I knew the word stool, but it had been used in a different meaning.

Another time, my family had gone to Estes Park, and we went to lunch. I was asked to order what I wanted. Well, I didn't speak English, but I had heard the word hamburger. So I ordered a hamburger. Well I sat there with the hamburger in front of me because I didn't know how to eat a hamburger. Our friend told me to pick it up and bite it. I wanted a knife and fork to cut it. On this day, I learned how to eat a hamburger!

AR-My dad did not speak English either. Upon his entry to the United States, he stopped in a restaurant to eat. He could not order in English, so he put up two fingers and ordered two tacos. He lifted two more fingers and ordered two more tacos. Since he was hungry, he thought of a way to order that didn't require speaking.

EO-I remember having two friends at my house. Lupe spoke only Spanish, and Dorothy spoke English only. So I had to translate what each one was saying in their language.

AR-My family lived in Medicine Bow, and my stepmother Lupe didn't understand English. Well I was only six years old and English was my primary language. We developed a system at the grocery store. She would ask me how much an item cost, and I would show her by counting on my fingers. For example forty-three cents, would be four fingers, and then three. How were you able to learn English?

EO-We spoke Spanish growing up in New Mexico. Rock River, Wyoming had a population of about 350 people and about 6 of us spoke Spanish.

One day I was at your house and Lupe asked you to get a can of *chicharos*, I was so happy because I thought she said *chicharones*. Just hearing the word *chicharones* made me smile. Well guess what, you got a can of peas. I had quickly learned a new word-*chicharos*. Do you know what *chicharones* are? It is a very delicious treat!!!

My Emma also had some trouble at school because she could not say *reloj*. She would come home and I would teach her the pronunciation. Rolling the r's caused her so much anxiety! I guess each day we can learn something new.

I spoke to my kids in Spanish, until they went to school and started learning English. You can say that we were learning English together. This sounds kinda strange, but I learned to read English by reading True Story magazines. I would read one story over and over till I understood the words.

AR-Today we have teachers in schools that teach ESL-English as a second language. A person can become isolated and not want to speak; why try when you can't be understood? Can you believe Elsie, we went through a time when they were trying to pass a law that said English Only would be spoken? It was like asking us to stop making tortillas!!!!

Elsie, how did you communicate with the teachers in Rock River? What about writing a note to the teachers? Discipline of seven children had to be constant. Did you have to go to school to discuss discipline problems?

EO-I learned how to be a parent from my sister Edda. She really didn't have to spank us, but what I remember the most is that she disciplined with love.

She took the time to explain her decisions. She knew the right words to say that lifted your spirit. She was not the type of person to say, "I told you so." We hear about bullying in schools, and kids being mean to each other. Where does all this start?

AR-I think about my grandkids and worry for them. We didn't experience the violence that we hear about today. The worst crime that I remember was when the boys put trash cans in front of the school and blocked the entrance.

The school was closed the next day, so they could clean up. This was a school prank, no malicious intentions at all.

There were three Hispanic families in Medicine Bow and everyone treated my family with respect. I didn't experience prejudice in this beautiful community. Today, we all are part of a community; our neighbors, the schools, the grocery store, the hospital. What do you think you contribute to your community?

One teacher took all of the students to her home, to watch her new color TV. Our teachers empowered us to believe that our dreams could be achieved, because each of us had potential. I didn't have all the fancy clothes, or the latest make-up, (blue eye shadow) but I always felt like I belonged. What do we become when we believe we belong?

EO-I think sometimes our own people are prejudice against each other. Maybe someone gets a new car, or house. We can't be happy for that person.

Just think of Selena and how her own friend killed her. Greed once again made its presence known. A person, who is mean, probably doesn't feel love for themselves. They give away what they have inside.

AR-I think people who are mean to others need to validate themselves by disrespect. It makes them feel superior by being a bully.

They need us more than we need them. Their existence depends on yelling, screaming, beating the person who is the closest. The person on the receiving end feels it is their fault. I had a friend whose husband would take her head and beat it into a corner cabinet. Why I asked, well because he could.

What Gives You the Right?

What gives you the right to hate, degrade, and shame?
Always needing to be right, and so full of blame.
You hurt me with your words, and leave scares on my
    heart, and this causes me to doubt in myself.

I guess I am not worthy of honor and respect?
What gives you the right to break a person's body and
    spirit?
My pain goes unspoken, my heart remains broken.

You silence my voice, and leave me no choice.
I can't trust what I feel, and wonder if my life is real.

What gives you the right to make demands, while you
    beat me with your hands?
How can you sleep at night? What you makes you think
    this is right?
It is time for all of us to tell you-we know the truth.
Many saw my tears, my scars, my wounded spirit, I
    don't need to speak.
What gives you the right to think, nobody would know?

AR- Here is another question for you Elsie. What shows did you watch on TV?

I love the title: Sand in the hour glass, these are the days of our lives. I can still remember the sand going thru the hour glass, and thinking wow, I hope my life isn't that short.

EO-I watched the Guiding Light as I folded laundry, or ironed. My kids loved American Bandstand, especially my girls. We didn't have too many choices; I think we had three channels. Today, a person can have about 100 choices.

But convenience has its down side also. Kids love to play with the remote, and look out for the dog chewing it. I remember those rabbit ear antennas, and they took a beating from the wind.

AR-I remember putting aluminum foil on our rabbit ears antenna because there was so much fuzz on the screen, or it would be rolling down the screen. The famous Zenith and Motorola, had a life of about 25 years or so. How would you decide who could pick a TV show?

EO-My kids didn't watch a lot of TV because they were outside, at school, or working. I do remember something very significant that we watched on TV.

United States of America experienced the assassination of President Kennedy. My Stephen was the first to alert me about the news. He was six at the time, and was home with me that day. I ran to the TV and put Steven on my lap.

The reality was in front of me in black and white. I immediately started praying and asked God to help our President survive. Well, we all know what happened; a nation was grieving for their president Kennedy. I could see the tears on people's faces. We hugged each other and honored the hope that he gave each of us.

AR-I remember going to your house, Elsie and Walter Cronkite was reporting the news. The kids were very aware of what Tom expected during the news broadcast! It was very quiet when Tom was watching Walter!

I also loved the TV show, The Rifle Man, and Red Skelton show. Not so much the shows, but the fact that I watched them with my dad, and we laughed together. The TV shows of today send mixed messages, like *Desperate Housewives.* I felt desperate when my kids were sick, or got their feelings hurt, or when I needed to figure out how to pay for their college education.

Another show is called, *Survival.* We had the bitter cold, and brought in coal and wood to keep warm. My dad always worked and we had plenty to eat, but survival had a different meaning.

EO- Casos de Familias is a show about families and their struggles. Our struggles were social injustice: the Vietnam War, equality in the work force, respect towards each other. We were searching for our identity within our community. Where did we fit in? Everything changes around us all the time. Today there is a lot of cussing and sex on TV. A person wants to make sure there are no children around to listen.

AR-Music was a great comfort to us because it became away of expression. We had one radio station that we listened to, and that was KOMA-from Oklahoma, City. They played all the greatest hits, and had song dedications. Some of favorites songs were: War- the words to this song asked some very relevant questions. War- what it is good for, absolutely nothing.

Crystal Blue Persuasion - words- All of his children, every nation. Anybody here- words - have you seen Abraham, Martin and John. Just songs that made us questions our beliefs and our place in society.

EO- Dancing to Mexican music is something that everyone knew about Tave. His brother was a musician and when he visited we knew it was time to dance. Polka type music was fast moving and a person had to be quick on their feet. My kids also had their favorite tunes along with a record player.

Sometimes Tave would want to play Mexican music, and he would find the record player. He would tell me that all he saw was monkeys, monkeys, monkeys. He was finding all sorts of records by the monkeys.

AR-Elsie, what is your favorite song?

EO-Well this is a song that has been around for a long time. It is called, *"Un Dia a laVez."* It is called one day at a time. The words remind us that all we really have is today.

I also have another favorite song-*She is a Goodhearted Woman.*

Tave and Elsie

EO- Tave and I met at a dance, in Greeley. My first thought of Tave, was that he would be a great brother-in-law, because he was around twelve years older than me.

My sister Edda was very protective of me and would not allow me to go anywhere by myself. Here we were at the dance, where I was wearing a beautiful two piece outfit my sister had purchased for me.

The jacket had star buttons on the shoulders. Tave came over and asked me if I was in the service. I actually saw stars myself. I did not tell anyone, though. We talked, not texted, or phoned!!! Conversation about everything in general. I was so amazed about his stories of being in the Army.

I remember a date we had, well sort of a date. He asked permission to go to the movies: Gone with the Wind -to be exact. Well my sister said yes, but my other sister also had to go. Well there we were at the movies. We did not sit together, but every now and then we glanced at each other. I have seen Gone With the Wind many times, and I smile and remember. It is a beautiful love story, and reminds me of my first date with Tave.

I called him Tave, because his family told me that his name was Octaviano. Everyone knew him by Tom.

AR- How long did you and Tom date?

EO-It was about a year, and you better believe that my sister continued her watchful eye over us. I know she wanted the best for me, and I saw her love for me through her strict rules.

I worked in the kitchen of a hospital. I worked part time and also attended school. My boss really appreciated my hard work, and would allow me time for my studies.

I found another job, which was really convenient. I could not believe the benefits. Tave's sister Connie and I were hired by Bonnell nursing home in Greeley. Neither one us could drive, so they gave us a bedroom, and we could stay there. To tell you the truth, neither one of us learned to drive.

I had my job, and school and was not concerned about being in love till I met Tave.

EO- After Tave's tour of duty he returned to Greeley, where his family lived. He worked as a farmhand and the owner of the farm was going to deed him some land, so he could manage it. Tave had been told about employment with Union Pacific. So he made his decision to move to Wyoming.

He would be paid $198 every two weeks. We did not question if we could live on $400 per month, much less raise a family of seven.

AR-Sometimes less information is better. Do you think it was love at first sight?

EO-Absolutely, there is no doubt. We had some time to know each other. Our love continued to grow as we raised our family. Each of us focused on our family. I mean he was working in the cold each day to put food on the table. It took both of us to raise our kids and help them sort through life's issues.

Since I came from big family and so did Tave, having a houseful of kids was normal.

AR- OK Elsie, I think I hear wedding bells, when did Tom propose marriage?

EO-He asked my sister and brother, and they said my dad Ezikel had to give his permission. He was out of town because he worked as a sheepherder. So a letter was sent to him. We waited to hear his answer.

He came home and talked to me. He wanted to know if I wanted to be married, and was Tave the man I wanted for a husband. I had to answer my father these questions, but he allowed me to speak for myself, and not influence me in any way. It had to be my decision.

Finally, my father gave his approval, and our family went into wedding planning. You would have thought we won the lottery!! The date was set - March 10th, 1948. Our family was old fashion, because the groom had to ask for his bride's hand in marriage. It is a beautiful tradition, which I cherish to this day.

My son David asked for his wife Betty's hand in marriage. I don't think it is old fashion as much as recognizing and honoring the bride's family. I don't know of families that teach their children this tradition.

We were married at our Lady of Peace in Greeley. Tave came from a family of musicians and just like that we had music for our wedding. Someone played the violin and guitar, I don't remember an accordion.

It was a very traditional wedding. We had our parents do *"La Entrega."* We sat down, and our parents came and gave us their blessings. In the background a song was played that said, *Goodbye my son, now you are a husband. Goodbye my daughter, now you are a wife.*

Friends and family surrounded us as our family blessed our marriage.

Elsie and Tom Olivas
1948

Quien Iva Saber

Quien iva saber, que nuestro amor nos junto en 1948?

Quien iva pensar que nuestras vidas ivan hacer unidas?

Quien iva saber que el amor no avisa?

Quien iva creer en el amor de primera vista?

Two cents worth: If you can't read Spanish, here is a hint- Amor means love.

My Wedding Gown

My wedding dress was a total surprise to me. Tave's parents went to Denver and purchased my wedding dress, veil, shoes, and a beautiful necklace.

The dress was all satin, with a flowing train. It had beautiful sculptured long sleeves. It did not have a lot of beading, but it glistened as I stood by the window. I wrapped the veil around my arm as I walked.

It was a surprise to me, that everything fit. My hair was styled, and I remember looking in the mirror at the future Elsie Olivas.

My family's emotions were in high gear....sheer joy.

Tave's family prepared the meal. Guests and family were plenty, since we both came from large families. I was so happy he became my husband and not my brother in law!

Wedding Veil Dilema

My wedding dress and veil where so beautiful. I wanted to preserve them forever.

I saved my veil in an escritorio-which was an antique desk. It was beautiful, and had little slots inside. I thought this was the perfect hide away for my veil.

The escritorio represented a place in history and so did my veil. You know how we are about keeping cards, and that first grade report card.

I was not hiding it, I was preserving it; I wrapped it up in tissue paper and remembered how I felt as a bride.

Anyway, through the years, of raising my kids, the veil lost its importance. One day Tave's sister came to visit and she really liked the escritorio. Tave teased her and told her he would sell it to her for $10. I was ok with the deal, after all it would stay with the family.

Well, many years later, I remembered what I had so carefully tucked away inside the escritorio. I felt sad because I didn't know what happened to my veil. Something I held in my hand, with such significance to me, would not mean the same to another person.

Today, I know that my veil was a gift, that I received, so what is freely received is freely given. That is what I think anyway. I am sure we have all lost something that had a heartfelt attachment.

AR- Oh yes, I have too Elsie. My dad asked me what I wanted for Christmas. I knew there wasn't a lot of extra money for presents. I wanted a watch. Well I got my watch - a Timex.

Each night I would carefully put it on my night stand and I would wind it for the next day. Just a simple routine.

Well one day walking to school in the snow, I lost my watch. I was crying and back tracking my path. What emotions I experienced. It was something that my dad bought me; he took the time to ask me, what I wanted.

It was a connection to my dad. I felt like daddy's girl when I put it on. Timex watches get my attention at the stores. I just glance over and remember.

AR-Marriage is so much work Elsie, you have to want to invest your time, energy, and lots of patience. We do get cranky, because of work, money, kids, cars, traffic, you name it.

Only today they say we are having mood swings, or we are whiners. Back in the days it was called cranky. Same emotion different name!!! They still say may the bride and groom live happily ever after. I often wonder -after what?

EO- Well we were married 51 years. Not everyday was happy. We had plenty of trials with seven kids. My kids did not have all the new clothes, or shoes, but I hope they know they were loved.

AR-Elise you planted the seeds. I see the love you have for Tom as you speak of him.

A Young Girl's Heart

Love came to a young girls heart
It was true love from the start.
In cold Wyoming we lived our life,
As I became Tave's wife.

Our trials were plenty,
Our children our greatest blessing.
Love of a lifetime, love one of a kind.
I hope you too will find.

What is in a Name?

We started our own family, and our first child was born. Tave and I decided to take turns naming our children. Our first child was Virginia, named after my mom.

Well our next baby was a boy, and the nurse kept asking for the baby's name. Tave told his sister that it was his turn to name the baby boy. Did she have any suggestions? Well his sister picked the name of Victor Andres.

Soon enough, we had another boy, and I named him after his dad, Thomas Clarence. A baby girl made her appearance in January, and it was my turn, and I named her Emma after Tave's sister.

David, our next son was named after a radio show that I listened to. The name of the show was called David and Sally Farrel. I just loved the name David.

Connie was named after Tave' sister. His sister is very special to us, and I loved the name Connie.

By the time Steven was born, Tave and I talked about names. We decided together, on Steven. We both said the name and liked how it sounded.

Our baby boy George got his name from a family friend. He told Tave that he called everyone George. Every family should have a George. So we named our son-George.

AR-It means so much to know why we have our name. I wonder Elsie, where your mom picked your name?

EO-Well she could of named me Memoria because I was born on Memorial day. I am happy that she didn't.

Some people change their names for personal reasons. How difficult it would be if you had known a person for twenty years and then they changed their name. It would be difficult to remember a new name and remember to use it.

Sign of the Times

AR- Elsie, today we have a remote for TV's, fans, radios, and toys. (Heaven forbid if we lose the remote, everyone knows about it.) We have the world at our fingertips. Not to mention, the washing machine, ice makers, (not the difficult metal ice trays) What did you need to maintain a family?

EO-I sure could of used a dryer; the bitter cold just went right to your bones. It wasn't like the clothes were going to dry, they always froze, instantly!

Well, I became the proud owner of a Maytag, and you would of thought I was the proud owner of a new Cadillac. It was so sturdy it lasted over 50 years and still works. We can't say that about too many appliances. It probably washed about 2000 or more loads of laundry.

AR- I remember helping Connie and Emma bring in the clothes from outside. The jeans were stiff as an icicle. I think you could of added a gallon of downy, and they would not of even bent, much less softened. Each day was filled with household chores.

FYI-Downey was invented in December 1961.

EO-I had to have a schedule for my chores. On Monday I washed clothes, Tuesday was time to iron. Friday was a day to sweep and mop, and clean. My friend and I had our theory about washing clothes.

We looked towards Rawlins and if it was cloudy, we would not do our washing because it would snow. If we looked towards Laramie and it was clear, we would have a good laundry day. Our forecasting system worked darn well for us.

We didn't tell anyone else, so our theory wasn't tested outside of ourselves, the inventors!!!

Groovy 1960

Politics	President Kennedy elected as President. Martin Luther King - I Have a Dream Speech War in Vietnam

Movie Star   Elizabeth Taylor   Best movie - James Bond

TV shows   Gunsmoke
                       Wagon Train   Bonanza The Brady
                       I love Lucy   Bunch

History   Cassius Clay (then) wins gold medal in the Olympics
Berry Gordy starts Motown with $800 loan
Neil Armstrong and Edwin Aldrin landed on the moon

Sports	Joe Namath- Football
	Mohammad Ali youngest boxer to win a title
	Jackie Robinson -first black major league baseball player
Economy	Eggs-.57 dozen Gas-.31 per gallon
	Postage .04
Songs	The Twist
	Loco Motion
Clothes	Mini and Maxi skirt
	Long vinyl boots
	Polyester suits
Music	The twist (no touching while dancing this dance!)
	Peter Paul and Mary
	The Beatles (Ed Sullivan Show)
	Elvis Presley still producing hit after hit

Wyoming Waits

Tumble weeds in Wyoming are blown by the wind all over the roads. Most people remember the wind, and can't remember a day without it.

The small town that we lived in provided a safe environment because we didn't lock our doors, and the kids left their bikes outside all the time. We didn't have a fear of them being stolen. I think today, our lives are ruled by fear.

AR-We lived in Medicine Bow, for fifteen years. I learned about genuine friendship-meaning a kind word spoke had no hidden motives. Our small town provided a foundation for safety and trust.

We always had food, shelter from the Wyoming winters, and friends we could count on.

We moved to Denver and my family was under siege. We were the only Mexican family in our neighborhood, and our house was surrounded by about ten kids who wanted to break in. This was in the middle of the day. My brother would insert knives across the locks to prevent them from breaking in.

We had never experienced such a violation of safety. I remembering running out the back door to ask our neighbors to call the police. How does a family prepare for this confrontation?

We had riots that spoke about Chicano Power. I had never heard that term. I had not identified myself as a Chicano, and what about the power part? Not sure what all the rioting was about.

In Wyoming I was allowed to be who I was, no power necessary. It was time to question where a family from Wyoming would fit in.

EO-We lived in Wyoming all of our lives; once the kids graduated, they had to find a way of making a living. They also left their safe surroundings. My kids belonged to the community of Rock River, which allowed us to be the Olivas Family.

Kids will be kids, and we always had a house full of guests. Tave and I bought a house for $4500. I could not believe that big number, but it meant we would have a house for our family.

Of course we made payments, and it was worth the sacrifice.

Our yard was huge, and we had a small like cabin towards the back of the house. I can remember looking out my window and watching my boys play Cowboys and Indians. Sometimes they were GI Joes and they would be crawling on the ground. This always made me smile as I watched through a window. The safety of a place called home.

AR-Elsie, I remember going with Connie and Jenny to an old abandoned house. We were on a treasure hunt. We imagined the people that had lived there, and what was cooking for dinner.

Out of nowhere, Connie saw the beautiful piece of glass in a corner. The sunlight scattered into 100 colors. We sat there looking at this beautiful broken glass and imagined drinking a cold soda with a straw inside. What imagination our town provided. I felt like we were on a field trip!

One of our favorite pastimes was walking to the school, and sitting on the swings and watching these huge semi-trucks go by. We would ask each other what far away places we would go if we could drive a semi-truck. Well we had one consistent winner-California to see Disneyland.

Next to the school was *The Longhorn Café*. The statue of a huge horse store stood proudly next to the café. We would take turns getting on the horse because we sat up high and our vision extended above the trees. Women with a vision brought to you by the horse in Rock River.

Family Stories

EO- I didn't worry about my kids being at the school, or going to the *Long Horn Café*. Connie and Emma were never alone, they had plenty of friends.

My boys were busy, working, or outside being mechanics with their dad. Tave used a stern voice when he wanted to make a point.

Tave did discipline, but he didn't cuss. His strongest words were, *By Golly.* When the kids wanted something he would tell them to ask their "nana." Of course there was fighting between the siblings; we were just as normal as everyone else!

One day a salesman came to our home selling melamac dinner ware. His sales pitch was that the melamac dishes would not break, since we had so many teenagers, I decided to pay attention.

Well, I decided I need a pair of dishes that did not break and Tave agreed to the purchase. I was so proud of my new dishes, and none had broken till one day, I heard a pounding sound outside.

Tommy had broke some plates with a hammer. He told me the salesman was wrong. I had to explain to him that dishes are to be used under normal circumstances-everyday use. Taking a hammer to them was not everyday use.

He was not breaking any rules, just my new plates. I told him that he could not break what was left of the dishes. I knew he was just curious, and how could I be mad at him? He was just testing the dishes.

AR-Our kids leave us with so many memories Elsie. I remember, my son Joseph was about seven when he acted out of pure innocence. We had some friends visiting and Joseph kept whispering to me. I was too embarrassed to repeat what he was saying, but our friends wanted to know. Well finally I told them that Joseph wanted me to ask our friend if he needed a comb because his hair was a mess!

I taught my oldest son to drive, but not without a few bumps along the way. He wore a size 13 shoe and the gas pedal was very small. Well I was determined to take him to the country where the traffic was limited.

Well, in the country he knocked down a whole row of mail boxes. So much for my theory!!!

EO-I have another story I want to share. We always had pets, which the kids took good care of. We had a Pekinese dog named Lady. She was normal in every way, but Victor gave her a very special job to do.

We had chickens and we enjoyed fresh eggs for breakfast each morning. Well, Victor taught Lady to roll the eggs to the front door without breaking them. Lady would bark once she got to the door.

I can still see Victor on the ground showing Lady how

to roll the eggs. It was incredible that she learned and never broke them.

I think that she could of easily been on a TV show!

My kids always teased each other, like all kids do. My Connie struggled to get on the school bus each morning. So she was called short legs. Go figure huh.

Virgie kinda had the same problem; she could not reach the gas pedal to drive a car. I remember when she was learning to drive and we came upon a ditch. Well, Tave told her to step on the gas pedal so we would not get stuck in the ditch.

She tried to step on the gas pedal but she had difficulty reaching it. Here was the Olivas family stuck in the ditch.

I insisted that we all go with Virgie on her driving lessons. I think it probably made her nervous to have at least eight people in the car!!

Some of the kids taught each other to drive. We couldn't afford a car for each of them, so they learned to share, and also to wait so they could buy their own vehicle.

It tested my patience to have seven teenagers driving. Our yard was huge, and I can still remember all these cars parked there. Don't ask me what our auto insurance bill was because I don't remember!!!

I didn't learn to drive myself because I had an abundance of drivers. We didn't go to far away from home. We had a grocery store in Rock River that extended credit to us. It was interesting because when pay-day came, we paid our bill off-and immediately charged groceries for two more weeks. No credit cards were necessary, and the best part, no interest to pay.

Laramie was about forty miles away, and so we would go there to buy our groceries also. The groceries were so much cheaper in Laramie, but with our larger family, we were always running out of something. We would of bought flour and milk by the buckets!!!!!

I do have a special memory of Tave and me. On this day Tave and I were talking about dying and where we wanted to be buried. Well Tave said to me that I could just throw him in the alley. Well I said, "No honey you aren't getting off that easy, I will bury you in the ground." He looked at me with that crooked smile of his.

The Double Shot Bar

Tave also had some special friends. He worked with Union Pacific and the workers and their families became our friends. The kids attended the same schools and the wives visited each other.

Sometimes we met at the Double Shot Bar in Rock River. I would go and sit with Tave, and would order a beer. I wasn't really a drinker but I was a paying customer.

AR-Elsie, what made you a brave woman?

EO- Well, one night, Tave wanted to go from Rock River to Medicine Bow and the roads were very icy. I told him I was afraid of the ice. He said I know if you drink a beer, it will make you brave. I decided I didn't need to be brave because the roads were to icy.

We didn't have dances, concerts, restaurants or Malls, so we made the best of our time at the Double Shot Bar.

Today you can rent movies or get on a computer. I guess we didn't know what we were missing!

AR-Today we have steak houses, Chinese take out, bakeries, Italian cuisine, fast food places, and Elise loves a sausage biscuit from McDonalds!

Family Time

Often times on Saturday, Tave would let me sleep in and he would fix the kids breakfast. I wasn't really sleeping, but just listening to my family cook with their dad. Sometimes he would fix eggs and at other times cereal.

Somehow they managed to clean the kitchen. He would tell them their nana needed extra rest. I had to agree with that.

Our house was not quiet very often, I don't know what I would of done.

My kids always had friends over; so it was a busy household.

What does the Thermometer Register?

EO- Winter months in Wyoming were often 20 degree's. Our railroad houses were not insulated, and the windows were glazed over with solid ice. It seemed like we were frozen inside of our houses.

We kept warm by a coal stove that was made out of cast iron It was in the middle of a room and stood proud like a ship at sea.

The coal stove had a pipe that was inserted into the wall. I don't think the pipe was very thick. We would warm ourselves by standing around the stove. Nearby we had our shoes drying out.

My boys hauled in buckets of coal and we felt secure knowing how toasty warm we would be. Tave would get up and stoke the fire, so when the kids woke up, the house was very warm.

AR-I often wonder what a thermometer would register as my father stoked the stove so much, it turned red. Perhaps it would of melted the thermometer!

Once the stove was red, our dad would go outside and bring buckets of snow. He would shovel snow into the stove to cool it off. We all sat around and watched as the snow sizzled into the red coal. What a sight for us to see. This process was repeated many times during the winter season.

EO-The heat from a coal stove doesn't compare to the heat of a gas stove. Our stoves were not inspected for safety, and we didn't have fire extinguishers.

One day, Tave tried to get a fire started, and was not being successful. Soon, our house was filled with smoke and the kids were coughing.

The wind was howling outside, and sparks were flying from the chimney.

Meanwhile, all the kids noses were black from breathing the smoke. We laughed at each other as we looked at our noses, but we were breathing some sort of fumes.

Well Tave discovered the reason the stove was smoking. Inside the pipes he found a dead bird. The kids were curious about the dead bird and forgot about their black noses!!!!! What if we would of been sleeping and the stove had been smoking?

This was a way of life for most of the railroad families. The coal stoves kept us warm all those winter months, for years. No maintenance was necessary. One thing for sure, it turned our walls black because of the smoke. During the summer it was time to scrub and paint. Once again, our hands and noses turned black.

AR-Today we are advised to keep fire extinguishers close, and our kids are taught fire safety at school. I think it is such a miracle that we didn't have families perish in fires.

I also think of the smoke damage to our lungs and carbon monoxide inside our homes.

We were so thankful to have heat, I don't think we thought about the fire dangers. Elsie tells me that Rock River had a volunteer fire department. Thank goodness no serious injuries came from fires. The potential was certainly there.

Favorite Past Times

EO- Bringing in coal and clearing snow didn't give my kids to many opportunities for boredom.

I don't remember our kids saying they were bored too many times. They were always building something, playing a sport, or listening to music, doing homework. I think it was when the kids were older that we would play cards.

I learned to play cards from my friend, Gregoria. She played solitaire for hours. You could tell she loved her card game and was more than willing to teach me.

Tave's sister would come over and also wanted to play cards. One thing for sure, we had a huge pot of coffee going during our card games. The coffee pot made about twenty cups of coffee and you better believe it we drank it all. (We could have opened our own coffee shop.) Now, it was up to you if you wanted to drink and gamble at the same time.

Our card games would go to 2 in the morning. Exhaustion would not stop us. It was a great way to spend time together. Plus, today we have these beautiful memories. It was a simple life, yet very rich in family relationships.

My family was quite competitive when it came to playing card games. Rummy was our favorite for awhile, and then we learned the game of hearts. My Connie was a gambler and wanted to challenge everyone to start with a $5 bet. Sometimes our bets were nickel Anne instead of dollar Anne!

AR- A favorite past time for us was playing kick-the-can, red rover, red rover, and hide and seek. I can still remember holding our hands so tight.

Something that Connie, Jenny, Emma and myself just loved to do was go riding around. Emma was the oldest and the one in charge. Our riding around consisted of going around the ditch about twenty times. Of course KOMA provided music for our sing along.

Emma did not have her driver's license, but life didn't get much better than driving around the ditch singing tunes to KOMA!!!

Today, kids entertain themselves with computer games. They watch movies on DVD's. Instead of listening to KOMA like we did, today an Ipod holds up to one thousand songs.

Can you imagine owning one thousands 45 records?

I can just see Emma, Connie, Jenny and myself hanging up clothes outside in the wind, but we are singing to the one thousand songs in our Ipad. It would probably take the chill out of that Wyoming weather.

What would we do with our little, static filled radios? Would we talk about our favorite songs, and write down every word?

EO-I don't know if this a favorite past-time, but it was necessary for me. I would take pleated skirts and remove the pleats. I would use the fabric to make sheets. My theory was to have one set of sheets to change, so when I washed I would have some clean ones.

Graduation time meant being creative with my resources. I would buy the boys used suits and come home and alter them to fit. I would take in the seams and measure and cut. I would iron creases into the pants.

The white shirts were soaked in starch and then I ironed them. Wrinkles were not visible to the eye!!!

People would admire my boys in their suits, and nothing made this nana smile more!!! Why one time my Tommy was asked to be an usher in a wedding because he looked so handsome in his suit.

Their shoes were polished and their hair held in place with brel-cream.

Facts

A&R- This brings to mind a comment I heard on the radio. One of Elvis Presley's songs-*I AM ALL SHOOK UP*- got its name from a can of pop. Someone handed a person in the room a pop, but it got shaken up. So, creativity took over and- *I AM ALL SHOOK UP* became a huge hit. (Who wouldn't get all shook up watching Elvis dance and sing this song!)

Flashback Time

1980

President	Jimmy Carter
Unemployment	5.8%
Median Income	$17,710
Cost of stamp	.15
Gallon of gas	1.25
Cost of dozen eggs	.91

Music	Working my Way Back to you
	Running Against the wind
	(We were all running against the
	Wyoming wind.)
Invention:	Rubiks cube and the cordless
	phone
News:	Mount Saint Helen's erupts
	John Lennon is shot
TV	Dallas, Dukes of Hazard, Little
	House on the Prairie
	Elsie has ashes from Mount
	St. Helen's.

Knowing Elsie

I have relished this experience of interviewing Elsie every two weeks. One thing I notice is that she always makes me laugh. I call with a list of questions to ask, but Elsie always asks how I am doing.

On this day we talked about how expensive a gallon of gas is. Elsie told me that Tom could travel from Wyoming to Greeley on $10 per gas tank. They bought gas on credit but Elsie put into practice what she learned from her sister Edda.

EO-Edda had told me that when you pay off a bill, don't go charge again. Well, Tave wanted to buy a lawn mower on credit and I decided we could wait, save the money and not pay interest.

The darn thing was $145, and we did pay cash. Of course it meant being diligent every month and cutting down somewhere else. We had a huge yard and this was a necessity. It was a beautiful lawn mower-probably because it was paid for!

Elsie's wisdom guided her to raise a family on limited funds, no driver's license, unlimited socks that didn't match, and a stocked pantry. She knew there was always enough.

She always knew that love multiplies and comes back a hundred fold. You hear it in her voice when she talks about her family.

Details of Our Lives

I had these interesting questions for Elsie, but her answers were not one yes or no; and they always surprised me .

AR- What are something that you have not done?

EO- I am afraid of flying, it really doesn't interest me at all. I have not gone to Las Vegas, Nevada. It really doesn't seem like something that I would want to do. My kids do enjoy gambling, and I don't want to know when they lose money.

AR-What would you like to do?

EO-Win the lottery, for sure. But Victor reminds me that if I don't play, my chances decrease from winning.

AR-Elsie, what is your favorite piece of jewelry?

EO- My wedding ring that Victor and David found. You know they were found in separate states. One in Colorado and one in Wyoming. Some women have a ring on every finger, but what happens when I make tortillas? Then I would have five or six rings full of masa.

AR-Elsie, What is your favorite T shirt and what does it say about you as a person.

EO- Well, I love my bronco shirt, I must get ready to put it on because the bronco's are playing. My favorite shirt says: *Denver Broncos.*

I do wish I would of learned to drive. Once all the kids learned to drive, I had at least five or six drivers. Living so far from Laramie worried me because of an emergency. I tell you we would have kept an emergency room busy!

AR- What famous movie star would you like to have lunch with?

EO- Gee I have to think about this one. Well if I had a choice it would be Clark Gable. He was a very handsome man. I don't know if I could eat because of my nerves. I would just want to look at him the whole time!!!

AR- I can just see it: Elsie Olivas spotted with Clark Gable dining at Wendys!!!!

EO-I also must tell you a very important fact about my kids. There are many Senior Citizens among them. I really don't want to mention their ages, or names!

I remember how worried I was about them being teenagers and watch them grow up. Here I am with Senior Citizens. I am so blessed.

AR- Well, being a senior citizen comes with some benefits.

We get discounts at some restaurants and other businesses are also catching on.

What about all those times we dyed our hair, and got a different shade? Wrinkle creams are not that cheap to buy. What about those shoes that we buy for extra support? (They are extremely heavy to walk in.)

What about those socks that have the rough bottoms so we don't fall? I recently watched a commercial about snoring products. What about all those darn vitamins?

How many pair of reading glasses have we lost? What about books in large print ? You will notice the large print of this book!

Who doesn't want to remain forever young? I congratulate each and everyone of you who has experienced any of the above, you are not alone.

Where does this Journey Take Us?

AR - I am honored in sharing this story about Elsie.

At times I wanted to cry with her, and at times we laughed together.

This is not the end of her story, because now you can call and ask her questions of your own.

May your life be filled with joyous hope; this is the greatest gift that Elsie has shared with me.

Her endurance through the heartaches, and her precious smile makes you want to give her a bear hug!

She reminds me of a familiar story of a man who had two sons. He gives them their inheritance and sends them out into the world.

The first son buries his money because he is afraid it would be stolen. The other son saves a part of it and uses his money to buy provisions for families, he helps orphaned children, and learns a trade. He invests his time and money very wisely.

Upon their return home the father asked both of the

about the treasures he gave them. The first son tells him that he did not lose it and he shows him 100% of his treasure.

The second son tells him that he helped children, took supplies to the farmers out in the field. He also came back with part of his treasure. He had multiplied his treasure, but not in money.

Elise has discovered her treasures, and has bestowed them upon each of us at different times. Her love comes through every word she speaks. Her treasures have multiplied and increased in each one of our hearts.

I encourage you to ask questions of your mom, dad, aunts and uncles. What does their favorite T shirt say? What about their favorite candy bar? What made them cry? What do they treasure in their hearts? What do you treasure in your heart?

For Elsie

I am so honored for this opportunity, to write Elsie's stories,

We laughed together, shared a meal, and wiped away tears.

Her memories are vivid, with colors, names and places.

She can even remember people's faces!

Her faith was apparent from the start, and her gift of love comes from a joyous heart.

She has cried plenty of tears, beginning with the death of her mom at the age of nine.

Enduring heartache, not giving up hope, believing in goodness is who she is inside.

I heard her stories about Tom, and the Wyoming cold.

A lifetime of memories of her children she told.

Her wisdom, compassion, and grace has taken hold.

He who gives his heart, gives all.-Gandhi

Elsie and Tom Olivas
1998

About Antonia

Antonia is a Colorado native with some detours to Alabama, Tennessee, and Florida.

Encouragement from a fourth grade teacher to write a paragraph everyday, has brought years of creativity and discipline to her writing. Writing is a freedom of expression of our dreams, hopes, fears and hurts. Through this process a person can become a bronco fan, have a date with Clark Cable at Wendy's, and eat as many of her favorite candy bars without anyone knowing!

Our words keep us in touch with who we are inside; opinion's of others are not necessary. These words become our experiences and we own them. What will you learn about yourself if you write one paragraph a day?

CPSIA information can be obtained
at www.ICGtesting.com
Printed in the USA
FFOW05n2227230913
1865FF